D1103988

KN

DEC 06

WASTE and RECYCLING

by Sally Morgan

A+

Smart Apple Media

First published in 2006 by Evans Brothers Limited
2A Portman Mansions, Chiltern Street, London W1U 6NR

Produced for Evans Brothers Limited by White-Thomson Publishing Ltd.
210 High Street, Lewes, East Sussex BN7 2NH

Editorial: Catherine Clarke; Design: Tinstar Design Ltd.; Consultant: Lisa Cockerton;
WWF Reviewers: Patricia Kendell and Cherry Duggan; Picture Research: Amy Sparks

Acknowledgements
Alamy **p. 38**; Corbis **pp.** 12 (Pitchal Frederic/Corbis Sygma), **13** (Galen Rowell), **20** (Rafiqur Rahman/Reuters), **23** (Tom Stewart), **26** (John Zoiner), **28** (Keren Su), **29** (Michael S. Yamashita), **34** (Strauss/Curtis), **41** (Macduff Everton), **45** (Jose Luis Pelaez, Inc.); Digitalvision **p. 36**; Ecoscene **pp. 6** (Erik Schaffer), **7** (Alan Towse), **8** (Vicki Coombs), **10** (Jon Bower), **14** (Bruce Harber), **16** (Wayne Lawler), **27** (Chinch Gryniewicz), **31** (Wayne Lawler), **32** (Tony Page), **33** (Melanie Peters), **37** (Luc Hosten), **42** (Peter Cairns), **43** (Bruce Harber), **44** (Kevin King); Photolibrary **pp. 15** (Workbook, Inc.), **17** (Photononstop), **18** (Index Stock Imagery), **21** (Lon E. Lauber), **22** (Mark Bolton), **25** (BSIP/OSF), **30** (The Image Works); Practical Action ITDG **p. 40**; Topfoto **pp. 9, 35, 39** (The Image Works); TRAID UK **p. 24**; WTPix **p. 4**.

Cover photograph reproduced with permission of OSF/Photolibrary/Images.Com.

Published in the United States by Smart Apple Media
2140 Howard Drive West, North Mankato, Minnesota 56003

Library of Congress Cataloging-in-Publication Data

Morgan, Sally.
Waste and recycling / by Sally Morgan.
p. cm. — (Sustainable futures)
Includes index.
ISBN-13: 978-1-58340-981-7
1. Refuse and refuse disposal—Juvenile literature. 2. Recycling (Waste, etc.)—Juvenile literature. I. Title. II. Series.

TD792.M66 2006
363.72'8—dc22   2005057615

9 8 7 6 5 4 3 2 1

Contents

The waste problem

As standards of living increase around the world, people can afford to buy consumer goods such as cars, refrigerators, cell phones, and televisions. The manufacture of all of these goods is using up the planet's resources faster than they are being produced, which means that supplies will run out. If this is to be prevented, it is vitally important that the world's resources be used in a sustainable way. The word "sustainable" means "the ability to continue to support itself indefinitely." A product can be considered sustainable if its production enables the resources from which it was made to continue to be available for future generations.

Around the world, people are producing more and more waste. Developed countries in Europe and North America produce far more waste than most other countries, although India and China are catching up. The least amount of waste is produced in countries such as Gambia and Tanzania in Africa. In the past, people were more likely to repair something than throw it away, so goods lasted much longer. Today, people tend to throw something away when it breaks, often because it is cheaper to buy something new than to have repairs done.

People buy numerous electrical goods for the home. Often, these items are replaced if they get damaged because it's cheaper to buy new than to pay for repairs. The design of some items can make repair almost impossible, so they have to be replaced.

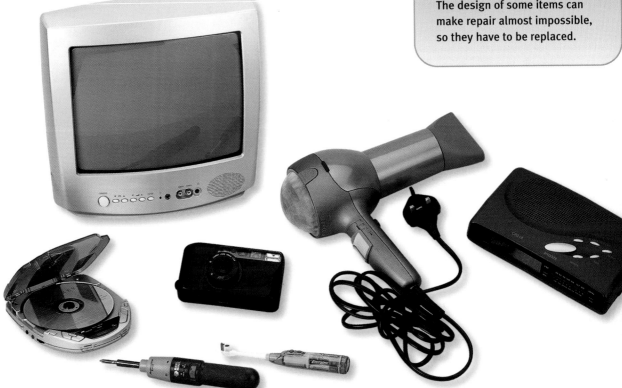

Life cycles

When looking for ways to reduce waste, it is important to consider the whole life cycle of a product. The life cycle starts with the raw materials and energy used to make a product, the energy needed to transport it, and, finally, the way it is treated after it is used and thrown away. For example, when we buy a plastic bottle of mineral water, we drink the water and throw away the bottle. We probably do not think about the raw materials and energy that were needed to make the plastic bottle, fill it with water, transport it and distribute it. We probably don't worry about what happens to it once it is thrown away, either. To get a good idea of the amount of waste we generate and its financial and environmental costs, it is important to consider the full life cycle of products and not just the time when they are useful to us.

Tackling waste

There is a phrase that people use to describe the ways in which the growing problem of waste can be tackled. This phrase is "reduce, reuse, and recycle." Reduce means to stop or avoid waste production. This can mean reducing the quantity of raw materials that are used in the manufacturing process or redesigning products so that they use less material. Reuse means to put an item to a

Recycled or not?

One symbol that is used on packaging in many countries to indicate that it can be recycled is a loop that consists of three arrows arranged in a triangle. However, recently, this symbol has been used to show that the product or packaging has been made using recycled materials. So the loop can mean both recycled content and that the product is recyclable. When a product is described as "recycled," it means that it contains material that has been reprocessed. However, this does not mean that it is made from 100 percent recycled material, so it could contain any proportion of recycled material.

new use, rather than to throw it away—for example, giving old clothes to a thrift shop, selling unwanted items, or repairing something so it can be used longer. Recycling is the processing of used items to obtain materials that can be used to make new products.

This pie chart shows the makeup of the garbage in a typical household in the United Kingdom (UK). Much of this garbage can be recycled or reused. In 2000, the people of the world produced 13.9 billion tons (12.6 billion t) of waste, which is 2.2 tons (2 t) for every person. By 2050, this is expected to rise to 29.4 billion tons (26.7 billion t), which will be 3.3 tons (3 t) per person! We all need to think of better ways of dealing with our waste before this happens.

paper 25%

kitchen and garden wastes 35%

plastic 11%

metal 9%

other 11%

glass 9%

Source: Friends of the Earth

Dealing with waste

People have always produced waste, but now there are more people making more waste than ever before. There are many forms of waste, including waste food, packaging, old electrical goods, broken household items, waste paper, and much more. Industries, too, create large quantities of waste during the manufacture of goods. Waste is even produced when raw materials such as coal and limestone are dug from the ground.

People and waste

Historically, most household waste has been dumped, buried, or burned. This method of waste disposal is still common in poorer countries, especially where there are large slums or camps with no organized waste collections or sanitation. The only way these people can get rid of their waste is to dump or burn it. In developed countries, waste is collected from houses and taken to landfills or incinerators. Part of the problem in the developed world is the ease with which waste is taken away. People do not usually see where their garbage goes or what happens to it. So in order to reduce the amount of waste, people have to be made to think about the volume of waste they generate.

In many countries, piles of burning garbage are a common sight. However, rotting food can attract vermin and spread disease.

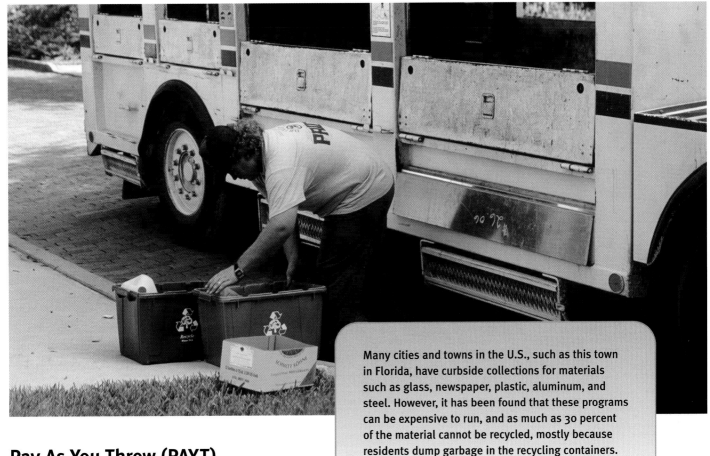

Pay As You Throw (PAYT)

Garbage collection is paid for through local taxes. In most places, everybody pays the same amount, regardless of the amount of waste they produce. This is beginning to change. In about 6,000 communities across the United States, there are Pay As You Throw (PAYT) programs that charge homeowners for their waste collection according to the amount of waste they put out for collection. Some programs charge for each bag or container of waste. Others charge according to the weight of the waste. These programs are designed to encourage people to produce less waste and to recycle more. In theory, it is a fair system because people pay for the garbage they produce. At first, there were concerns that people would dump garbage to avoid paying for its collection. However, in most of the places running the PAYT programs, this has not been a problem.

Getting people to recycle

If people recycle as much of their waste as possible, part of the waste problem can be solved. For recycling to be a success, however, it has to be easy to do, or convenient.

Examples of this include doorstep collections, in which homeowners put out items for recycling in special bins or boxes, and recycling bins on street corners and at stores. Recycling points that are placed in more remote locations are usually restricted to people who have cars. It is important that people do not have to drive out of their way to recycle their garbage and in doing so waste gas and add to harmful emissions in the atmosphere. Also, there needs to be a demand for the recycled items. There is no point in recycling vast quantities of glass or paper, for example, if there is no end use for them.

A highly successful recycling program has been running in Curitiba, Brazil, since 1989. The "garbage that is not garbage" program has been joined by 10,000 families. They each receive four and a half pounds (2 kg) of food for every nine pounds (4 kg) of recyclable garbage they deliver to mobile recycling units. Approximately 66 tons (60 t) of paper are recycled every day, which is like saving 1,200 trees that would otherwise be cut down.

A materials recovery facility is a central collection point for household waste. The useful parts of the waste, including aluminum and other metals, cardboard, and plastic, are removed and recycled. The remainder may be burned to generate electricity or taken to a landfill site.

Industrial waste

Turning raw materials into products makes waste. This waste includes that from both agricultural and manufacturing industries. Agricultural waste consists of things such as pesticides; empty pesticide containers; plastic wrapping, bags, and sheets; packaging waste; old machinery; oil; and waste veterinary medicines. Manufacturing waste depends on the technology used, the type of raw material processed, and how much of it is thrown away at the end of the process. Each stage of the production process generates a specific type of waste. In general, there are three groups of manufacturing waste:

- waste from extraction and transformation of raw materials, such as soil and rock in quarrying
- waste from manufacturing and production of goods (including building construction), such as leftover plastics, metals, and unused mortar from building walls
- waste from distribution and consumption of manufactured goods, such as packaging, pallets on which goods are moved, lengths of plastic, and wire.

There are ways of tackling this waste problem. Some involve governments making specific laws about waste, but others are voluntary programs undertaken by individual companies to reduce, reuse, and recycle their waste and to develop their business in a sustainable way.

There are official environmental standards that companies can meet. These standards show the public that the company cares for the environment and help the company gain a good reputation with its customers. For example, the international standard ISO14001 requires a company to establish an environmental policy and to consider how its products or services impact the environment. Worldwide, about 89,000 companies have achieved this standard. There are several advantages for a company that changes its business practices to meet this environmental standard, including an increase in efficiency, a reduction in the use of energy and raw materials, and the production of less waste.

Producer pays

Increasingly, laws are being passed around the world to make producers or manufacturers of products and packaging responsible for their recycling. This is often referred to as "producer responsibility." The laws encourage companies to make their products with minimal use of raw materials, to produce products with longer life spans, and to recover and recycle the products that are thrown away by the consumer. The European Union has applied "Extended Producer Responsibility" (EPR) to packaging, vehicles, and electrical and electronic products. Surprisingly, the U.S. has no federal laws (laws that cover all states) concerned with producer responsibilities, although a number of states have laws, and some companies have voluntary programs in place.

Green design

The term "green design" describes the various techniques used when considering the environment at each of the design stages of a product or system. The goal of green design is to conserve or minimize any damage to the environment. All products have some environmental impact, but some use more resources, cause more pollution, or generate more waste than others. Using green design helps to identify those that cause the least damage. For example, a green design can be achieved by using products that contain recyclable materials and recycled content, and by using the least toxic materials and manufacturing processes. It is also important to minimize or remove any unnecessary parts and to ensure that the product can carry out its function for as long as possible. There are now more requirements for manufacturers to take back products, such as computer equipment, at the end of their life. This has encouraged manufacturers to consider designs that can be taken apart and recycled.

> "Once companies realize that they are going to have to pay for waste management and recycling, they have an incentive to make less wasteful products and to design for recyclability by reducing the materials and parts used, particularly reducing the number of different plastics, labeling them, and designing fasteners for easy disassembly."

Spokesperson for a U.S.-based environmental research organization

> "Extended Producer Responsibilities (EPR) on packaging has become too complex in Europe."

Publisher, Recycling Laws International, U.S.

Having a working lunch is common today, and office workers eat prepackaged foods at their desks. This practice generates large quantities of waste in the form of plastic cups, paper napkins, and cardboard and plastic packing.

What are incinerators?

Incineration is a common way of disposing of waste. The waste, both household and industrial, is burned at high temperatures. The waste product is an ash that is disposed of in landfill sites. Incinerators provide a convenient way of getting rid of waste, but there are both advantages and disadvantages to their construction.

Incinerators are expensive to build, at approximately $404 million each. The most recent ones have very strict emission controls, using filters in their chimneys, and incorporate a waste-to-energy plant that generates electricity for local homes and businesses. In some areas of the world, incinerators play a central role in waste management. For example, on Long Island, New York, as much as 50 percent of household waste is burned in 5 waste-to-energy incinerators. Often, it is more efficient to burn wastes such as mixed plastics, which are difficult to recycle.

Harmful emissions

There have been problems with emissions from incinerators. The Baldovie incinerator in Scotland, for example, had to be shut down because the emissions contained high levels of the toxic chemical dioxin, which came from burning PVC (a type of plastic). Sometimes the ash contains high levels of heavy metals such as mercury and lead. Removing PVC plastics from the waste could reduce the dioxin emission problem.

However, a major source of PVC is hospital waste, and this needs to be incinerated for health reasons. Hospitals could be encouraged to work with reusable equipment rather than disposables and to purchase non-PVC alternatives, but these tend to be more expensive.

This incinerator in Hong Kong, with smoke pouring out of its chimneys, has been built close to a residential area. The emissions from the chimneys drift over the area.

Electricity from waste

Incineration does not solve the problem of waste. In fact, it tends to encourage people to continue to produce waste because it can be burned. Waste-to-energy plants need waste with a high content of plastic, paper, and organic matter. This is because these materials contain a lot of carbon, which releases heat when it is burned. The heat is used to generate electricity. Incinerators need a steady stream of waste to keep the generators going, so they tend to compete with local recycling programs, with waste being burned instead of recycled.

Recycling instead

As landfill sites fill up, the real alternative to incineration is recycling. In both developed and developing countries, recycling generates more jobs and less pollution and is more sustainable than incineration. In Europe and North America, there are a range of high-tech industries springing up that deal with making products from recycled materials, while in the developing world, recycling projects are creating jobs for the poorest members of society. It must be remembered, however, that there is still an environmental cost to recycling, although it is much less than using raw materials.

Waste fact

Choosing to recycle, rather than burn, waste saves energy. Recycling paper saves three times the energy than that gained by burning, plastic five times, and textiles six times.

> "Landfilling is becoming more expensive, and waste-to-energy plants have improved. It really requires a fresh look."

Member of an environmental research group

> "Incineration is inconsistent with reduction, reuse, and recycling because it relies on a steady, large quantity of mixed waste. It is a superficial solution that does not attack the root of the problem—we must waste less."

Ruth Grier, Government Minister for the Environment, Canada

All forms of waste disposal create jobs for people, but recycling programs are labor-intensive and create far more jobs than a landfill operation. This can be important in countries where there are high levels of unemployment.

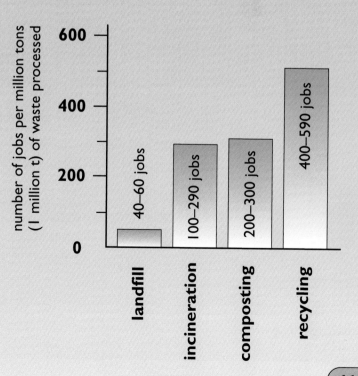

number of jobs per million tons (1 million t) of waste processed

- landfill: 40–60 jobs
- incineration: 100–290 jobs
- composting: 200–300 jobs
- recycling: 400–590 jobs

type of waste processing

Source: Friends of the Earth

CHAPTER 3

Glass

The first glass dates back to 4000 B.C., when it was used to make jewelry. Since that time, it has been used in a wide range of objects, including containers for cooking and drinking. Today, glass is a very common material. It was one of the first materials to be recycled, and now a large percentage of all glass bottles and containers are recycled.

Making glass

Glass was an expensive material until the 1800s, when the mass-production of glass containers began. Today, the raw materials are more readily available, so it is fairly cheap to make. Glass is made from three main ingredients: sand, soda ash, and limestone. The ingredients are added together in a furnace and then heated until they melt. The molten glass is then poured into molds or blown to make bottles or other containers. Glass-making needs a source of heat, which is usually produced by burning fossil fuels.

Newly made bottles in this glassworks in France are automatically filled with liquid. France recycles just over 50 percent of glass bottles, in particular the green glass used by the wine industry. Nine out of 10 champagne bottles are made from recycled glass.

Reducing and reusing bottles

There are ways of reducing the amount of glass needed. Modern bottles, for example, are much lighter than in the past, and this saves on manufacturing and transportation costs. Just five years ago, a small beer bottle weighed nine ounces (260 g), but this has now been reduced by almost a third to six ounces (170 g).

Once a bottle has been used, it can either be reused or recycled. From an environmental point of view, it is much better to reuse a bottle than to recycle it. Less energy is used in the collection, cleaning, and refilling of a bottle than is needed to recycle it.

During the 1950s and 1960s, it was quite common to take bottles back to stores, from where they would be collected and taken back to the factory. As the manufacturing plants became larger and began to supply bottles to farther-away places, it became too costly to take the bottles back to the factory, so this practice slowly died out. In the UK, milk is still delivered to some homes in bottles. The average milk bottle is used about 20 times. In the developing world, reusing glass bottles is more common, and soft drinks and beer often come in glass bottles that are collected and returned to the factory.

Clear glass containers such as jam jars are frequently reused in homes for jam-making and pickling, among other things. However, a bottle or jar that is to be collected from homes or stores and reused many times has to be made from heavier, thicker glass in order to withstand wear and tear. Because of this, more glass is used in its manufacture and more energy in its transportation. There are also the additional costs of collection, transportation, and cleaning.

These crates, stacked in a street in Phalenksangu, in the Nepalese Himalayas, are full of empty soft drink bottles, which will be taken back to the factory for cleaning and refilling.

Recycling glass

The great thing about glass is that it can be recycled very easily, and this can happen over and over again without any loss of quality. Glass was the first material to be regularly recycled, and today a large percentage of all glass is recycled. In Finland and Switzerland, for example, as much as 90 percent of glass is recycled. Glass collected from factories and bottle banks is taken to recycling plants, where it is monitored for purity—that is, if it's all the same color, with no foil or caps—and crushed to make cullet. Then the cullet is mixed in with the other raw materials and melted.

Environmental benefits

Recycling has a number of environmental benefits. First, cullet melts at a lower temperature than is needed to make glass from raw materials, so this saves energy. Second, if this energy source was a fossil fuel, this reduces carbon dioxide emissions. Even after transportation and processing, every ton (1 t) of cullet melted saves 68 pounds (31 kg) of carbon dioxide. It also reduces the need for raw materials that have to be taken from

the ground. Limestone quarries can be located in attractive settings and often spoil the natural landscape. Recycling glass reduces the need to quarry for limestone and prevents this kind of damage.

Still thrown away

Despite the fact that glass is easy to recycle, much of it still ends up in garbage cans and landfills. One large source of this glass is bottles from bars and nightclubs. These businesses sell large numbers of bottles each night, and only a small percentage is recycled. Although the UK recycles more than a million tons (1 million t) of glass per year, glass still makes up seven percent of the average garbage can contents in the UK. In 2001, more than two and three-quarter million tons (2.5 million t) of glass ended up in UK landfills. Currently, UK households recycle just 34 percent of container glass.

This Danish supermarket has a "money-back" machine. People drop a bottle in the top and receive a small payment in return. This money encourages people to recycle their bottles.

One problem with recycling glass is that it comes in different colors. When the different colors are mixed, the recycled glass has a lower value because there are fewer uses. There is a shortage of clear glass, which is the most useful. In the UK, much of the recycled glass is green glass from wine bottles. These bottles have been imported from other wine-producing countries, and there is only a small market for recycled green glass in the UK. Usually, the green glass cullet is exported back to the country it came from for recycling.

Case Study: Successful recycling in Switzerland

In Switzerland, 90 percent of all glass bottles sold are recycled. In a few areas of the country, this figure is as high as 93.8 percent. Switzerland's amazingly high recycling figure has been achieved in a number of ways. First, there are glass banks everywhere, so people do not have to travel to recycle their glass. There are collection points in stores, too. Switzerland is a very clean country with hardly any litter on the streets, so recycling is also part of people's national pride. At school, children are taught to respect their environment, and they are encouraged to recycle. Children are taught rhymes to help them remember to recycle.

New uses

Recycled glass can be used in a number of ways. The most common way is to make new glass bottles and jars. In recent years, however, a number of new products that make use of recycled glass have appeared. These include the use of glass as decorative garden paving, in mosaics, and in jewelry. Glass can also be used as a filtrate to remove impurities from water. The construction industry is also a major user of recycled glass. Construction companies use it to make glasphalt, which is a type of road surface that contains 30 percent recycled glass. Glasphalt can be made with all different types of glass mixed together.

At this recycling plant, this huge pile of empty glass bottles is ready to be recycled and made into new objects or containers.

Metals

Metals are materials with valuable properties. For example, steel is strong and long-lasting, while lead is more flexible and can be bent into shape. These properties mean that metals are very useful, and there are few materials that can replace them. As developing countries become more industrialized, the use of metal increases. Currently, the industrial expansion of China and India is causing shortages of metals such as copper, iron, and steel, which are all used in construction. This shortage is pushing up the cost of these essential metals. Reducing the world's use of metals will be difficult, so the emphasis has to be on reuse and recycling.

Extracting and recycling

Most metals are extracted from the ground as ores. Ores are the rocks that contain the metals. For example, aluminum occurs in an ore called bauxite, while mercury occurs in cinnabar. The ores contain other substances, too—for example, most iron ores contain sand, rock, and silica. The metal ores have to be crushed and then processed to remove any impurities. This processing usually requires a lot of energy and generates considerable waste, as well as pollutants such as sulfur dioxide, which is one of the gases responsible for acid rain. Iron ore, for example, is refined in a blast furnace, and the waste products include slag, which is a mix of limestone and impurities from the iron ore, dust, and gas.

Metal objects are easy to recycle. The metal is simply heated until it melts and then molded into a new shape. Metals can be recycled over and over again with no loss in quality. In fact, there is so much metal already in existence that it could be possible not to have to extract any more ore from the ground.

This huge quarry in the rain forest of Papua New Guinea digs out metal ores that contain copper and silver. The quarry is located on the side of a hill, and it creates huge piles of waste. The high rainfall means that water carries silt into local streams and rivers.

Most of the valuable metals can be recycled, including steel, copper, aluminum, lead, tin, zinc, gold, silver, and platinum. Today, about 45 percent of all steel and nearly 40 percent of the world's copper come from recycled sources. However, some metals have to be recycled by specialist processors. For example, gold and platinum can be recovered from old electronic equipment such as computers, but the process is complex and hazardous to health, as these metals are harmful if inhaled (as vapor) or if absorbed through the skin.

Why recycle?

There are several benefits of recycling metals. By not having to extract ores from the ground, there can be fewer quarries. Quarries are not only unattractive to look at, but they also produce a lot of waste soil and rock. Often, this waste is dumped in piles around the quarry. Large vehicles have to carry the ore from the quarry, creating dust and traffic problems and using fuel. Recycling means fewer quarries and less air pollution. Ores are often transported long distances because some metal ores, such as bauxite, are found only in certain parts of the world. Bauxite is shipped from Australia to North America and Europe.

This man in Botswana is reusing aluminum cans as a building material to construct a wall. In the developing world, the lack of resources can mean that people are more imaginative about what can be done with "waste" materials.

This transportation can be avoided if metals are recycled. Metal ores have to be processed, and this uses more energy and creates more waste than melting down and reusing metal.

Percentage of steel packaging (such as drink cans and other containers) that is recycled

Steel cans are very easy to recycle, and the metal is valuable, but even in countries that top the chart for steel recycling, only 6 out of every 10 cans are recycled.

percentage recycled

country

Japan — U.S. — Australia — New Zealand — Europe (average) — Switzerland — Italy — UK

Source: U.S. Environmental Protection Agency

Using aluminum

Aluminum is a shiny, strong, malleable metal that can be rolled very thin. It is also lightweight, so it is ideal for making items such as drink cans, aerosols, folding chairs, and ladders. It is the preferred metal for drink cans, as it keeps drinks fresh, cools quickly in the refrigerator, and can be crushed and recycled. In 2001, more than 200 billion cans were sold around the world. To meet this demand, the current world production of refined aluminum is in excess of 19.8 million tons (18 million t) per year.

Making aluminum

Aluminum is obtained from bauxite ore. Bauxite is unsustainable, because one day it will run out. There are huge bauxite quarries in countries such as Australia and Jamaica. A great deal of energy is needed to quarry the ore, transport it around the world, and then extract the pure metal. Making new aluminum objects from recycled aluminum is much easier. Aluminum is melted down and shaped into ingots. The ingots can be stored until needed. When they are heated, they can

Case Study: Cash for cans

Aluminum is a valuable metal, so collecting cans is a great way for organizations and schools to raise money for charity. About 50,000 cans weigh 1 ton (1 t), and when they are crushed, they take up about 140 cubic feet (4 cu m). There is a network of companies across Europe, Australia, and the U.S. that run "buy back" centers where people can take their cans and swap them for cash. Two charities in the UK—Alupro and Tree Aid—have joined forces to sponsor tree planting in Burkina Faso, in western Africa, with the money raised from recycling cans. The leader in aluminum can recycling is Brazil. In 2004, more than 16,000 schools, day care centers, and institutions in Brazil exchanged aluminum cans for more than 14,000 items, including electronic equipment, furniture, school kits, and food baskets.

These children in Brazil have collected aluminum cans from a beach. The cans will be crushed and sold to a scrap merchant.

be rolled and shaped into new objects. This process requires far less energy than making the metal from bauxite. Recycling results in savings in transportation costs, pollution, and quarrying. Worldwide, about 50 percent of aluminum cans are recycled.

Reducing use of aluminum

There are ways of reducing the amount of aluminum being used. Today, empty aluminum cans weigh about .5 ounces (14 g), which is about 30 percent less than they weighed 25 years ago. This means that there are considerable savings made both in the amount of aluminum needed to make the cans and in transportation costs.

It's not just aluminum cans that can be recycled. A slightly different form of aluminum is used in tinfoil, bottle tops, and baking sheets, and these are all good sources of aluminum. The recycled aluminum from these sources is used by the car manufacturing industry for casting engine blocks and cylinder heads. This aluminum is actually an alloy, which is a mix of

at least two elements, one of which must be a metal. This changes the properties of the aluminum, and it means that this aluminum must be kept separate from aluminum cans.

Aluminum facts

▸ Recycling 2 pounds (1 kg) of aluminum saves up to 17.6 pounds (8 kg) of bauxite, 8.8 pounds (4 kg) of chemical products, and 14 kilowatt-hours of electricity compared with extracting the metal from bauxite.

▸ Twenty recycled aluminum cans can be made with the energy it takes to make one can from raw materials.

▸ Aluminum transfers heat almost two and a half times faster than iron. This means that heat is lost and gained through aluminum very quickly, so it is ideal for cooking and as a cold drink container.

▸ It's easy to tell a steel can from an aluminum can: a magnet will stick to the steel can but fall off the aluminum one.

Source: Waste Watch

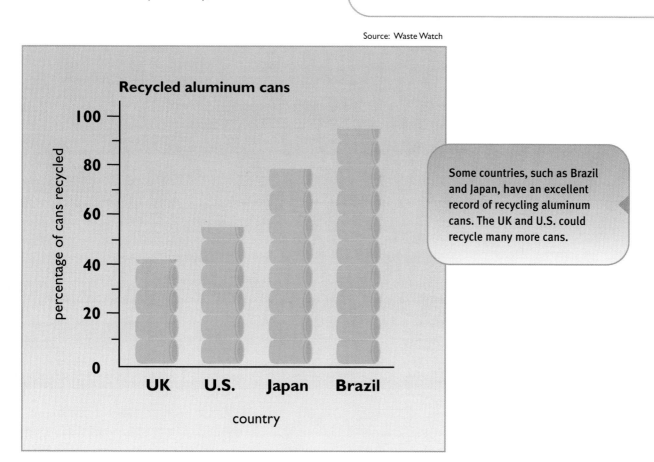

Recycled aluminum cans

percentage of cans recycled

100 — 80 — 60 — 40 — 20 — 0

UK   U.S.   Japan   Brazil

country

Some countries, such as Brazil and Japan, have an excellent record of recycling aluminum cans. The UK and U.S. could recycle many more cans.

Plastics, textiles, and paper

Plastics, textiles, and paper are all incredibly useful materials. These materials are all around us—in plastic containers, our clothes, newspapers, and magazines. Some of these materials are sustainable if used properly; some can be recycled and others reused.

Plastics

Plastic is extremely versatile, and vast quantities of it are manufactured each year. It is a popular packaging material because it is lightweight but strong and can be clear so that consumers can see the contents. Although it is useful, a lot of plastic ends up in landfills. It does not weigh as much as other forms of waste, but it is bulky and can take hundreds of years to break down, if it does at all.

Using plastic

There are pros and cons to using plastic. The use of plastic can help to conserve other resources. Plastics are lightweight, long-lasting, and can be shaped easily. These features enable manufacturers to do more with less material. This is known as source reduction. Source reduction is the process by which a package or product is made using fewer resources, creating less pollution and using fewer ingredients. Source reduction can also involve an improvement in the functionality and durability of a product.

These Bangladeshi women and their children are paid to sort plastic bottles into different colors and types at a recycling center in Dhaka, Bangladesh.

Since plastic is lightweight, it can be used to make large containers that would be too heavy for consumers if they were made from glass. Also, it requires less fuel to move the containers from the factory to the store. Plastics can take up less space, too. Paper bags take up seven times more space than the same number of plastic bags. So, one truckload of plastic bags would mean seven trucks if the bags were made of paper. Although these features help the environment, it must be remembered that not all plastics are easy to recycle, which means they end up in landfills or incinerators.

Saving energy?

There is no doubt that plastics can save energy. Studies in the U.S. looked at the energy required to manufacture, use, and dispose of common packaging items, such as bottles, tubs, and wraps, and compared this with the most likely nonplastic alternatives. By using plastic rather than the alternatives, product manufacturers in the U.S. would save enough energy each year to power a city of one million homes for more than three years. However, plastics are manufactured from fossil fuels, especially oil. Fossil fuels are unsustainable resources that are quickly being depleted. In addition, fossil fuels release carbon dioxide when they are burned, and this carbon dioxide is contributing to global warming. The way forward may be to make plastics from natural oils obtained from plants such as oil seed rape. Oil seed rape and other oil-producing crops could be grown on a much larger scale, but governments would need to encourage farmers to grow these crops and to invest in new equipment.

Plastic facts

▶ Plastic production uses eight percent of the world's oil. About four percent of this oil is used as a raw material and four percent as an energy source for the manufacturing process.

▶ In India, use of plastic is four and a half pounds (2 kg) per person per year. In European countries, it is 130 pounds (60 kg) per person per year, and in the U.S., it is 175 pounds (80 kg) per person per year.

▶ In India, cows are allowed to roam freely. Unfortunately, as many as 100 cows die each day after eating plastic bags that they find littering the ground. Plastic litter is a problem in South Africa too, where studies showed 90 percent of blue petrel chicks on Marion Island (off the coast of South Africa) had plastic in their stomachs, fed to them by their parents.

Plastic bags can be carried by the wind and get trapped on trees and fences. Besides being unsightly, they can also be a threat to wildlife. This fallow deer has plastic caught on its antlers.

Reducing and reusing plastics

The best way to tackle the problem of plastic waste is to reduce the amount of waste that is produced. This can be achieved in a number of ways. Manufacturers and stores can avoid using unnecessary packaging. Shoppers can reuse heavy plastic bags to carry their shopping, rather than pick up a new bag each time they buy something. Plastic bottles can be reused or put to some other use instead of being thrown away. There is a market for quality second-hand plastic containers that can be put to a new use—for example, large, heavy-duty plastic containers can be reused as rain barrels or feed containers for livestock. Some of the quality plastic components in cars can be removed and reused.

Recycling plastic

Plastics can be quite difficult to recycle, because many plastic items are made of several different types of plastic. The different types have to be separated before they can be recycled. Plastic bottles can be recycled because they are made from one of only three types of plastic, and this can be identified easily. Some plastic packaging is made from blended plastic, which cannot be identified so easily. The blended plastic is usually burned in an incinerator rather than being placed in a landfill. Different types of plastics can be identified from the number or code that appears on them inside a triangular recycling symbol. However, the presence of this code does not always mean that the item can be recycled easily.

These plastic bottles are being reused as mini cloches. These are used to protect young plants from being killed off by bad weather, such as frost, before they have the chance to develop. This is just one example of how plastic can be reused—can you think of any others?

The plastic bottles and containers are sorted, cleaned, and then shredded to form granules. These granules are melted down and molded into a new object. There is an increasing range of recycled plastic objects, including plastic plant pots, boots, decks, and benches. Plastic bottles made from PET (see table below) are particularly useful because the plastic can be used to make egg containers, new bottles, fiber filling for quilts, carpets, rugs, and even fleece jackets. PVC is used to make pipes and electrical fittings. Currently, the demand for recycled plastic in many countries is greater than the supply, so there is plenty of reason for people to recycle more.

All sorts of amazing products can be made from recycled plastic bottles, including fleece jackets! It takes just 25 2-liter soft drink bottles to make an adult-sized fleece jacket.

Different types of plastics

Symbol	Type of plastic	Properties	Use
PET	polyethylene terephthalate	rigid, clear or green	soft drink bottles
PVC	polyvinyl chloride	semi-rigid, glossy	squash and mineral water bottles
HDPE	high density polyethylene	semi-rigid	milk bottles and fabric softener bottles
LDPE	low density polyethylene	flexible	bread bags, plastic bags
PP	polypropylene	semi-rigid	margarine tubs, screw top lids
PS	polystyrene	brittle and glossy	carryout packaging, foam cups
OTHER	multilayer plastics	squeezable	ketchup and syrup bottles

Textiles

Every day, we use a wide range of textiles, including curtains, carpets, and clothes. Many of these are made from fibers such as cotton, wool, linen, and sisal. All of these textiles can be recycled, but many just get thrown away and end up in landfills.

Reusing textiles

One of the main problems today is the number of cheap clothes that are being sold. Low prices mean that people are more likely to throw old clothes away and buy new ones than to alter and reuse them. However, there is a secondhand market for more expensive designer clothing and items such as carpets and curtains. These textiles are sold in secondhand stores.

Efficient recycling

Textiles are very efficient to recycle because textile reprocessors are able to recycle as much as 93 percent of textiles without producing any harmful by-products or wastes. When the textiles arrive at the recycling center, they are identified, graded, and sorted. This is a highly skilled job because the workers have to be able to identify a type of cloth or textile in seconds. Any good-quality clothing and shoes are removed and sent to thrift shops or exported to developing countries. For example, sneakers with little wear are sent to countries such as Bangladesh, where goods of such quality are often far too expensive or unavailable. This leaves the worn or damaged textiles, which can be cut and made into industrial wiping cloths. Any textiles that are unsuitable for making into cloths are used for other products. For example, woolen or cotton clothes can be unraveled, and the threads can be woven into new clothes or blankets or used for filling mattresses. Some of these reclaimed fibers may be used by companies to make new designer clothes.

TRAID (Textile Recycling for Aid and International Development) is one organization that makes new, recycled clothes out of unwanted clothes that have been donated to them. The new clothes are fashionable, as well as environmentally friendly, and the money raised from selling them goes to fund international projects for sustainability.

Case Study: The diaper story

A baby will have approximately 2,000 diaper changes a year and use up to 6,000 disposable diapers until potty trained. In a household with a baby, disposable diapers can make up 50 percent of the household's waste. Once in a landfill, disposable diapers swell in the rain. Consequently, they make up between two and eight percent of landfill volume.

A disposable diaper is made mostly of plastic, with some wood fibers. After it has been used, it is usually wrapped in a plastic bag and thrown away. A used diaper may be full of human sewage, too, so dumping all of this untreated sewage in landfills is not very healthy. It would be far better if the content of the diaper were put into the sewage system to be treated properly. Disposable diapers are quite expensive, too. In some countries, such as New Zealand, disposable diapers are imported, and this has further environmental costs of transportation.

So what is the alternative? The answer is "real" diapers made from natural fibers such as cotton. A real diaper can be washed and reused many times over. One argument against real diapers is that they are not as easy to use, and they are not waterproof. However, the latest real diapers look very similar to disposable ones as they are shaped and come with a waterproof outer cover that can also be washed. Since they are reused, these diapers only have to be purchased once. However, they do have to be washed at high temperatures, so there is an environmental cost from the washing machine, which will use electricity, water, and detergent.

Disposable diapers such as this one may seem harmless, but they are a huge contributor to the waste problem.

Paper

Most paper is made from a sustainable source—trees that can be harvested and replanted. As long as more trees are planted than are cut down, the process is sustainable. Fast-growing trees, such as spruce, fir, and eucalyptus, are planted for paper production.

Making paper

Making paper starts with wood chips from the harvested trees. The chips are placed in pulp digesters, where they are broken up by steam and chemicals into a pulp of fibers and other components of wood. These extra components, such as resin and lignin, are removed by further processing, leaving a pulp of pure fibers. The pulp is mixed with water and chemicals to form a mushy mix that is spread out and rolled to make paper.

If you look at paper with a microscope, you will see that it is made of long fibers. Better-quality papers have longer fibers. Paper is a relatively straightforward material to recycle because old paper can be mixed in with the pulp. Each time paper is recycled, however, the fibers get shorter, and this reduces the quality of the recycled paper. The lowest grade paper is used for newspapers.

Saving paper

Each year, large volumes of paper waste end up in landfills, mostly in the form of packaging and printed materials. Some of this will be contaminated with food and glue, and therefore it cannot be recycled. One way to reduce the amount of paper in landfills is to reduce the amount of paper that is used and thrown away. Paper can be saved in all sorts of ways—for example, by not printing out unnecessary sheets of paper from a computer, using scrap paper as a notepad, and using both sides of a sheet of paper before throwing it away. Businesses can reduce the paper they use by sending e-mails rather than faxes and letters, and sending some documents and reports electronically rather than printing them out. White office paper should be kept separate from colored or glossy paper when recycling.

At the end of the paper-making process, the paper is passed through a series of heated rollers that press and dry it. Finally, it is turned onto a huge roll and moved to the cutting room.

Recycling paper

If paper has to be thrown away, it is important to make sure that it is recycled. Usually, the different types of paper—for example, newsprint, magazines, cardboard, and office paper—are kept separate because each type has a different length of fiber. Waste paper does not have to be recycled into new paper. Paper can be shredded and used for animal bedding or building insulation.

Some types of paper and cardboard are difficult to recycle, especially waxed corrugated cardboard containers used for food. However, this can be composted. The paper and cardboard are shredded and placed in large compost bins, where worms, fungi, and bacteria break it down. The resulting compost can be sold for use in gardens.

Paper facts

▶ In the U.S., paper recycling averages 340 pounds (154 kg) a year for every person. This has increased from 234 pounds (106 kg) per person per year in 1990.

▶ In the UK, newsprint is made from 75 percent recovered fibers, although this figure varies from year to year.

▶ In 1989, there was only one mill in Canada capable of making newsprint with recycled content. Today, there are more than 25 such mills out of 150.

CHAPTER 6

Cars and e-waste

The market for consumer goods is huge and growing rapidly. In the modern world, people do not keep items such as cars, televisions, videos, phones, or computers for very long. New models with enhanced features continue to appear, and there is a huge demand to have the latest gadget or mobile phone. It is often costly or impossible to repair modern electrical goods, so it can be easier to buy new products. The increasing number of consumer goods being sold is producing large volumes of waste in the form of "old models." Much of this waste has to be specially treated.

Cars

The number of cars in the world is increasing, particularly in countries such as China and India. In 1990, there were just 1 million cars on Chinese roads, but by 2004 this had risen to 12 million. A further increase of 2.4 million new cars occurred in 2005. If these increases continue, there could be a staggering 140 million cars by 2020.

Cars have considerable environmental impact. Car manufacturing uses a great deal of raw materials, such as steel and aluminum, as well as energy. In addition, new cars may be transported around the world. While they are being driven, cars use energy and produce pollutants. Finally, at the end of a car's life, it is scrapped. The life span of a car has gotten shorter. In the past, cars were kept for 20 years or more; now, it is common for cars to be scrapped after just 10 years or so, especially those that have been involved in accidents.

Although car ownership is still relatively uncommon in rural areas of China, in cities such as Beijing, traffic congestion is becoming a problem. If car ownership continues to grow in China, there will be damaging consequences for the environment.

At recycling centers like this one in Japan, the useful parts of cars are removed and reused before the bodywork is crushed and recycled.

Recycling cars

As much as 75 percent of a car can be recycled, and there is no reason why this figure cannot reach 95 percent. It used to be just the metal frame of a car that was saved, but modern salvage yards are far more organized. Now, all the useable parts of a car are removed and sold as spare parts. This includes engine parts, plastics, and even the interior light bulbs. Strict rules in many countries require old cars to be taken to specific sites where they can be scrapped, and, in some cases, the car owner has to obtain a certificate of scrapping to prove that the car was not just dumped. Car manufacturers are under greater obligation to be responsible for the recycling of old cars, so they are beginning to change car designs in order to make recycling much easier.

Leaving the car behind

Recycling old cars does not really solve the problem of more cars being manufactured and the increasing use of gas to fuel them. As traffic congestion around the world gets worse, governments are looking for ways of persuading people to leave their cars behind and use public transportation instead. Some of the measures being taken to encourage drivers include:

- road or congestion charges
- high taxes on car purchases, ownership, and fuel
- cheaper public transportation.

In Beijing, China, the rise in private car ownership is creating smog and severe traffic congestion, so the city is introducing measures such as a fuel tax, high parking charges, and tighter regulations on exhaust emissions.

"If each Chinese family has two cars like U.S. families, then the cars needed by China, something like 600 million vehicles, will exceed all the cars in the world combined. That would be the greatest disaster for mankind."

Chinese environmentalist (Liang Congjie)

29

E-waste

Advances in technology have brought with them a new type of waste—electrical and electronic waste, or "e-waste." This type of waste barely existed 20 years ago. Now, e-waste represents the biggest and fastest-growing manufacturing waste. As products are continually invented and updated, the life of the old ones gets shorter, and the waste problem gets larger.

Not only is there a large quantity of e-waste, but it is also difficult to recycle because the equipment itself is made up of many different materials. The percentage composition varies, too. For example, a television contains about 6 percent metal and 50 percent glass, while an oven is 89 percent metal and only 6 percent glass. There are other materials, too, such as plastics, ceramics, and heavy metals.

The main component of e-waste comes from large household appliances, such as refrigerators, freezers, and washing machines, known as "white goods." They make up just under half of the total e-waste. The next largest component is information technology (IT) equipment, at 39 percent, most of which is computers. Recently, there has been an increase in the number of televisions and computer monitors being thrown away due to the arrival of new plasma and flat panel screens.

Recycling computers

Millions of computers are thrown away each year, and you would think that much of this waste could be recycled. Unfortunately, this is not the case, as just 50 percent of a computer is recycled, and the rest is dumped. The major problem with computers is that they contain toxic heavy metals such as lead, mercury, and cadmium. A computer can contain as much as four and a half pounds (2 kg) of lead, and this is difficult to dispose of safely. In addition, much of the plastic in a computer contains a flame retardant, which makes it difficult to recycle.

These cell phones may only be a few years old, but already they are on the garbage pile. Smaller, lighter phones, as well as those with built-in cameras and MP3 players, have taken the place of these old phones.

Most developed countries have strict rules regarding the disposal of computers because of the toxic metals they contain. This makes computer recycling very expensive. Some companies avoid the problem by shipping old computers to poorer countries. There, local people who are desperate to earn money take the computers apart. It is not uncommon to find entire communities, including children, earning their living by scavenging metals, glass, and plastic from old computers. To extract a small quantity of gold, the capacitors have to be melted down over a charcoal fire. The plastic on the wires is burned in barrels to expose the valuable copper wires. The total value of the metals in a computer is about $5. The people who do this are risking their health because the burning plastic releases dioxins and other toxic gases into the air. The rest of the computer is worthless, so it is usually dumped nearby, where the remaining heavy metals contaminate the ground.

Case Study: Computers for the developing world

In today's world, computers are common, and they have become a vital piece of equipment in schools, hospitals, offices, and stores. They are also becoming more numerous in the developing world, where more people are gaining access to the Internet. There are several charities, such as Computer Aid, that supply computers to people in the developing world. They take old computers from individuals and companies, repair and update them, then send them to schools and other organizations. This way, the life of the computer can be extended, which is more environmentally friendly than recycling. There can be problems, however. These refurbished computers can break, and when this happens, there is little technical support, so the computer often ends up on the scrap heap.

Facts about e-waste

▶ The manufacture of a new computer and monitor uses around 530 pounds (240 kg) of fossil fuels, 48.5 pounds (22 kg) of chemicals, and 400 gallons (1,500 L) of water.

▶ About eight ounces (230 g) of gold can be recovered from one ton (1 t) of old cell phones.

▶ Discarded monitors and televisions are probably the largest sources of lead in landfills. The cathode ray tube found in most computer monitors and television screens contains four and a half to six and a half pounds (2-3 kg) of lead.

These old computers in Australia are ready to be auctioned. Most of these computers will be bought for schoolchildren or by college students.

These old refrigerators are waiting to be recycled. The coolant is drained out, filtered, and reused, the insulating foam is removed, the oil is drained for recycling, and the metal body of the refrigerator is shredded and recycled.

Refrigerators, freezers, and CFCs

Today, most homes in the developed world have a refrigerator and probably a freezer. These electrical appliances were relatively rare in developing countries, but now ownership is increasing worldwide. Refrigerators need a coolant to carry the heat from the refrigerator so that the inside stays cool. In the past, chemicals called CFCs (chlorofluorocarbons) were used.

CFCs and ozone

For 50 years or so, CFCs were considered to be miracle chemicals. They were excellent coolants and solvents, and they were used in aerosols, cleaning products, and refrigerators and freezers. However, once CFCs are released into the air, they destroy ozone molecules. Ozone is found in a layer high in the atmosphere, where it has an important role in stopping harmful ultraviolet light in sunlight from reaching the ground. During the 1980s, it was noticed that, particularly above the Antarctic, CFCs and other chemicals were depleting the ozone layer. Countries in the southern hemisphere, such as Australia and Chile, reported higher levels of ultraviolet light, which has led to more cases of skin cancer and eye cataracts. CFC is also a potent greenhouse gas. Each molecule of CFC has the same effect as several thousand carbon dioxide molecules. This means that a slight increase in the concentration of CFCs in the atmosphere can cause a great deal more heat to be trapped, resulting in the rise of global temperatures.

Government action

Global concern over the damage being caused by CFCs led to most countries signing the Montreal Protocol in 1987, which was an agreement to phase out the production of CFCs and closely related ozone-destroying chemicals. A few years later, CFC production was completely banned, and no more CFCs were used as coolants. However, there were many millions of refrigerators and freezers containing CFCs already in existence, and these needed to be disposed of carefully to prevent the escape of CFCs into the atmosphere. In 2001, therefore, the European Union required CFCs and related chemicals to be removed from refrigeration equipment before it could be scrapped. This involves draining the cooling system and removing all of the insulating foam.

Reusing refrigerators and freezers

One way to reduce the number of refrigerators and freezers being scrapped is to remove the CFCs from old refrigerators and freezers and then restore them to working order using new, CFC-free alternatives. In many countries, there are organizations that train young people to refurbish old appliances. Sometimes old refrigerators and freezers containing CFCs are shipped to developing countries for resale. This is not always a good idea, however, because when this equipment finally stops working, it may be abandoned, allowing the coolant to escape.

CFCs

Since 1987, more than 150 countries have signed the Montreal Protocol, which called for a phased reduction in the release of CFCs. In January 1996, a complete ban on CFCs came into effect. Even with this ban, CFCs will continue to accumulate in the atmosphere for another decade. It may take until the middle of the next century for ozone levels in the Antarctic to return to the levels of the 1970s.

These secondhand refrigerators are for sale in Serrekunda, Gambia. They have been bought from European countries and may contain harmful CFCs.

Cell phones

The number of cell phones worldwide is rapidly increasing, even in remote parts of Africa. At the same time, the production of phones with new features, such as built-in cameras and MP3 players, is persuading many people in the developed world to replace their cell phones once a year. Sometimes people have to change their phone when they change providers. Not surprisingly, there are millions of discarded cell phones making up about one to two percent of e-waste. This may seem like a small amount, but phones contain toxic chemicals such as arsenic, cadmium, antimony, beryllium, copper, nickel, and mercury.

These chemicals are used in the manufacture of components such as the rechargeable battery and the LCD display. Therefore, cell phones can contaminate the environment if they are not disposed of carefully. There are now programs through which stores collect old phones and donate the money raised from their recycling to charity. Phones are refurbished and sold to countries where the latest technology is not so important to consumers. Also, most cell phone manufacturers have signed an international agreement to develop environmentally sound ways of dealing with end-of-life phones.

Cell phone facts

▶ Each year, an estimated 130 million cell phones end up in landfills or incinerators in the U.S. In the UK, about 15 million are thrown away in a year. In addition, there are probably hundreds of millions of old cell phones lying in drawers and cupboards around the world.

▶ National phone companies in Europe and North America have joined with charities to make a donation of between $1 and $90 for every cell phone they receive. For example, 10,000 recycled cell phones can pay for a guide dog for life.

Cell phones are used around the world, sometimes in unexpected places. This man in Botswana, for example, is talking on a cell phone.

Reducing e-waste

As with other materials, it is possible to reduce the amount of e-waste. It would not be necessary to replace a computer so frequently if it was possible to upgrade the computer chips and repairs were easy to carry out. Computer designers could consider ways of reducing the number of cables and boxes that are attached to a computer and to concentrate on designing computers that have built-in accessories, which would reduce the use of raw materials.

Computers use a lot of consumable items such as printer cartridges. Most inkjet printer manufacturers design their cartridges so that they cannot be refilled, which means that the consumer has to buy new ones. Inkjet cartridges could be refilled easily, and this would reduce waste. Other cartridges cannot be refilled, and these have to be returned to the manufacturer. Usually, the packaging of a new cartridge contains a prepaid label so that the cartridge can be returned for recycling in the box that came with the replacement cartridge. Toner cartridges, for example, can be returned to a factory, where they are completely dismantled and cleaned, any worn parts replaced, and the drum either re-coated or replaced. They are then refilled with fresh toner.

There are now laws in the European Union, known as the Waste Electrical and Electronic Equipment Directive (WEEE Directive), that are changing the way manufacturers deal with e-waste. As with packaging and other forms of waste, it is now the responsibility of the companies that manufacture or import electrical products to take back the products at the end of their "life." These companies are required to have collection points where users can return their old products free of charge.

"I talk to a lot of people who say they just want to make phone calls. They don't want to get e-mail or download ringtones or take photos. They don't need a new phone."

Spokesperson for the Wireless Consumer Alliance

"This new program encourages the recycling of mobile devices known to contain toxic materials and therefore ultimately helps the environment. At the same time, it has the added benefit of raising money for worthy organizations."

Spokesperson for a cell phone recycling company

The WEEE man is a huge robotic figure made up of scrap electrical and electronic equipment, displayed in the UK. It weighs 3.6 tons (3.3 t) and stands 23 feet (7 m) tall. It represents the average amount of e-waste thrown away by a person in the developed world in his or her lifetime.

Waste and the developing world

In most developing countries, especially those in Africa, there is more reuse and recycling than in the developed world. In part, this is due to different ideas and cultures. Also, there is more poverty, so people cannot afford to throw away and replace old goods if there is any way to reuse them.

Urban versus rural

Cities in many developing countries are usually large, sprawling places. Often there are extensive areas of very poor housing and squatter camps where people have no services such as electricity, water, or sewage. There is little waste collection, and there are large open dumps where garbage is burned. Waste is often a big-city problem. In rural areas, there tends to be less waste, and much of it is organic waste, such as food and sewage, which can be composted.

These people are picking over the garbage in a huge landfill in Manila, in the Philippines. A few are wearing gloves, but most have no protection on their hands or legs.

This young boy in South Africa is playing with a toy made from old wires and plastic wheels.

Waste scavengers

In cities in Asia, Africa, and Central and South America, many people make a living by sorting through huge waste dumps. They are called waste scavengers or ragpickers. They tend to be people who have moved to the city from the countryside looking for jobs and are most often women and children. These people experience very dangerous working conditions and handle hazardous waste without physical protection. For example, many work without gloves or thick-soled shoes. However, their role is very important because they recycle a significant proportion of the waste. This reduces the amount of waste, increases recycling, and creates jobs and wealth. The valuable job carried out by these people has been recognized in some cities, and they are now beginning to get better pay and working conditions. In countries such as Colombia, Brazil, and Argentina, waste scavengers are grouping together to form cooperatives in order to get a better price for the materials they collect.

Many of the items collected by waste scavengers are made into new goods that are then sold. The range of goods that can be made from waste is incredibly varied. Oil cans are made into lamps; wire and small wheels can be shaped into toy cars for children; metal containers are flattened and used as a building material to make new homes.

The life of a waste scavenger

▶ Two percent of the people who live in cities in the developing world make their living by scavenging in garbage dumps.

▶ In Mexico City, the life expectancy of a waste scavenger is 39 years, compared with 67 years for the rest of the population.

Problem tires

In many parts of the developing world, such as India, Pakistan, and southern Africa, old tires are a massive problem. Sometimes these tires are disposed of by being burned, which causes air pollution. Often the tires are just dumped by roadsides or in the countryside, where they trap pools of water. Malaria is a disease found in many developing countries, and the mosquitoes that carry malaria can breed in these small tire pools.

Fortunately, the recycling of tires has improved, and tires are becoming too valuable to throw away. Small businesses are springing up to collect, reuse, or recycle tires, and this is creating new jobs. One way to extend the life of a tire is to retread it. Tires are discarded because the treads have been worn down and the tire no longer grips the road. Old treads can be removed and new ones stuck on. Some of the heavier tires for trucks can be retreaded three to six times.

Alternatively, whole tires can be reused as tree guards, plant pots, and even crash barriers on roads. Tires can also be taken apart and put to various uses. For example, in Karachi, Pakistan, tire collectors remove the treads and cut them into thin strips to cover the wheels of donkey carts. The walls of tires can be cut and shaped into items such as soles of shoes, slippers, car windshield wipers, and bike pedals. The bits of rubber can be broken into "crumbs" that can be put to low-grade uses, such as rubber flooring, noise and vibration insulation, roof tiles, and road surfacing.

Old tires can cause serious pollution if they are dumped or burned. It is much better for the environment if the tires are reused or recycled in some way. These sandals for sale at Mahoney market in Tigray, Ethiopia, for example, have been made using the rubber from old tires.

Case Study: BMW and the Plastics Federation in South Africa

German car manufacturer BMW has set up plastic recycling programs in South Africa. During the manufacture of cars, many small bits of plastic are produced that could be recycled. However, the bits are in different colors, sizes, and types of plastic, which means they need to be sorted first. BMW has joined up with the Plastics Federation of South Africa to train jobless people to sort the plastics into different types to sell to recycling companies.

The program has proved to be so successful that it has been expanded to include the plastic waste from local schools. Plastic recycling has created many jobs and educated school children about the importance of waste management. More recently, BMW has sponsored green cages—recycling points in towns—where the public can take plastic. All of the plastic waste is taken to central collection points in BMW factories for baling, weighing, and storing.

Dumping waste

There is a growing problem of richer countries disposing of their waste in poorer countries. There are strict rules regarding the disposal of waste in countries of the European Union, North America, and Oceania, so some businesses find that it is cheaper to export their waste to countries where the rules are less strict. For example, computers and printer cartridges are exported to China, where unprotected workers break them up and retrieve the useful bits, exposing themselves to hazardous chemicals.

In recent years, many pesticides have been banned because they are too dangerous to use. When this happens, manufacturers have to destroy any stocks they have. It is often cheaper, however, to ship the pesticides to poorer countries, especially those in Africa. Today, there are huge stockpiles of dangerous pesticides, some of which were dumped as long as 40 years ago. They include harmful chemicals such as DDT, aldrin, dieldrin, and chlordane. These countries are unable to dispose of the pesticides safely, so the stockpiles remain.

In Dhaka, Bangladesh, this nine-year-old girl works seven days a week recycling batteries. She knocks open batteries with a hammer to recover the coil. Without any proper safety equipment, this job is a highly polluting and possibly cancer-causing activity.

CHAPTER 8

Organic waste

One of the simplest ways of dealing with organic waste, such as vegetable scraps from the kitchen and plant waste from the garden, is to put it on a compost heap. Here, the waste is broken down naturally by worms, slugs, snails, and microorganisms such as bacteria and fungi. The resulting material can then be put back into the garden as a natural fertilizer for the soil. Animals produce a lot of waste in the form of dung, and this can be an incredibly useful fuel. In many developing countries, cow dung is collected and shaped into flat rounds and sun-dried. Then the dung can be burned to provide heat for cooking.

Biogas

Biogas is a mix of gases, including methane, that can be burned for cooking and to provide electricity. It is an important source of sustainable fuel. It is made from the organic wastes of animals and people as well as waste food. The organic waste is dumped into an underground container, where the materials rot and release gas, which is then collected.

The waste slurry left in the pit is removed and used as a fertilizer on crops. Biogas digesters do not smell and are a hygienic way of using the wastes. Also, five times more energy is obtained from the waste using a biogas digester than from burning an equivalent quantity of animal dung.

This biodigester provides electricity for a whole school of children. The waste is put into the underground chamber (bottom left), where it breaks down and produces biogas. This is piped away and used as fuel to generate electricity for lighting and running school equipment.

Biogas has other benefits. It has created jobs for the women who collect the dung and other wastes and who sell the slurry as fertilizer, and for men who build and maintain the digesters. Many remote villages were without electricity before the arrival of biogas. Now, the electricity generated using biogas can power many rural businesses. There are environmental benefits, too. Biogas has replaced firewood as the main source of fuel, so the forests are being conserved. Also, women have more time. Before, they would have spent many hours each day collecting firewood. Biogas is a much cleaner fuel to burn than either dung or wood, so there is less air pollution.

Biogas on a larger scale

In 1981, the Indian government started a project to install biogas digesters in the rural parts of the country. Now there are more than two million, most of which supply biogas to just one household. There are also several thousand larger plants that supply whole villages. It is only recently that the developed world has recognized the potential of animal wastes and biogas. Large-scale biogas digesters using agricultural waste have been built in countries such as the Netherlands, while there are dung-burning power stations in the UK and U.S.

Vermiculture

Another way to break down organic household waste is to use worms. Worms are decomposers—animals that feed on organic matter and, in doing so, help to break it down and release nutrients back into the soil. Vermiculture (using worms) is very popular in Japan, where more than three and a third billion tons (3 billion t) of earthworms are imported each year for vermiculture projects.

These small, red worms are used in vermiculture because they grow quickly and eat a great deal of organic matter.

Case Study: Baobab fish farm, Kenya

Fish is an important source of protein in many developing countries. Fish such as tilapia can be bred in fish farms to provide a regular supply of food for local people. One such farm is Baobab fish farm in Kenya. The fish need a constant supply of clean water, but water is often in short supply. Baobab farm has found a way of cleaning the water so that it can be recycled back into the ponds. The wastewater from the fish ponds is full of nutrients that are needed by plants, so it is channeled to a series of beds where water-loving crops such as rice are grown. The plant roots take up the nutrients. The water that drains out of the crop beds is clean enough to be used in the fish pools again. This way, water is recycled and the crops are fertilized by a waste product. More than 90,000 people visit Baobab fish farm each year, and farmers in many parts of East Africa have set up similar sustainable systems, which are ideal for small farmers and villages.

Looking to the future

The world cannot continue to use raw materials and produce waste at the current rates. In general, people living in cities produce twice as much waste as people living in the country, mostly due to their dependence on prepacked goods. Two-thirds of the world's population lives in cities, and this number is growing rapidly, so the waste problem is going to get even worse. Many of the raw materials come from unsustainable sources, while the wastes may take many years to break down and may even produce toxic by-products. Landfills are filling up. It is essential, therefore, that the world addresses this problem and finds ways of reducing, reusing, and recycling waste. The waste problem cannot be solved overnight, and it will need to be approached in many different ways.

Zero waste

Today, most manufacturers produce goods in a way that is described as "cradle-to-grave." This involves the manufacture of a product from raw materials, the product's use, and its final disposal. A more sustainable approach is called the "cradle-to-cradle" system. This system involves manufacturers working together. The waste products of one manufacturer become the raw materials of another, eliminating as much waste as possible. This is more like the cycles found in the natural world, where the wastes of one organism are broken down and used by other organisms.

Using sustainable materials

Another way forward is greater use of sustainable sources for making materials such as plastic. It is possible to make plastic from the oil of plants such as oil seed rape. In fact, plants produce a range of different oils that could be put to many uses. It may even be possible to alter the plants genetically using gene technology to make them produce specific oils for particular purposes. However, some people may have concerns about the long-term environmental impact of such changes.

Oil seed rape produces seeds that have a high content of oil. This crop is usually harvested to make cooking oils and margarine, but, increasingly, the oil is made into biodiesel for use in vehicles.

More durable goods

People should be encouraged to keep their belongings for longer and not to replace consumer items such as phones, computers, and televisions every few years. It has been found that longer guarantee periods encourage people to have products repaired rather than buy new ones. Therefore, a purchase tax could be charged on electrical goods sold with less than a five-year repair or replacement warranty. There could be laws requiring manufacturers to include a certain percentage of recycled content in their products in order to increase the demand for recyclable materials. Taxes could be introduced on materials that cannot be recycled.

Governments could lead the way by making suppliers meet higher environmental standards. Government purchasing has brought about a program in Japan that requires buyers to think "green" when making purchases. In the UK, government departments have plans for using recycled paper products and hybrid vehicles to reduce the use of fossil fuels. Hybrid vehicles have engines that are powered by a rechargeable battery and fuel, rather than just fuel. They are among the least polluting and most fuel-efficient vehicles on the road.

Closing the loop

It is important to remember that recycling has not actually taken place until we buy or use products made from recycled materials. For recycling programs to be successful, there must be a demand for recycled waste. This demand is created when people buy recycled goods. In addition to helping the environment, buying recycled goods encourages investment in new industries, and this creates new jobs. The process of buying recycled goods is called "closing the loop."

Case Study: Torop eco-village

The eco-village of Torop lies to the north of Copenhagen, Denmark. It was set up in 1990 and is home to about 150 people who live in houses that are visually striking and varied, and made from either renewable or recycled materials such as timber, straw bales, and mud. All of the houses are well-insulated and make good use of solar energy. The goal was to create a community that included homes, stores, schools and businesses, a wind turbine, and organic food production so that the community could be self-sufficient. The village has its own biological wastewater cleaning system and gets its electricity from a 450-kilowatt wind turbine. Denmark now has a number of similar projects, known as urban ecology projects.

The distinctive shape of the dome houses in Torop reduces both the materials required to build the house and the heat loss by 30 percent. The large, south-facing windows let in light, and a wind turbine produces electricity for the homes.

What you can do to help

Taking action for the sustainable use of resources and reducing waste is becoming increasingly urgent in the 21st century. It is too easy to throw away materials that could be recycled. It is important that everybody thinks about recycling in order to reduce the amount of recyclable materials such as garden waste, glass, and metal that end up in the garbage can.

We can all help to reduce waste by making simple changes in our lives. Having a compost heap in the garden where you can place kitchen and garden waste is one change you can make. Recycling as much garbage as possible is another.

Organic matter such as kitchen waste and weeds from the garden can be dumped on a compost heap, where natural decomposers, such as fungi and bacteria, will break it down.

Thinking about your shopping

There are many things you can do to reduce waste when you go shopping. First, take a bag with you rather than picking up new plastic bags at every store you go into. Look carefully at the containers in which products are placed. Choose products in containers that can be recycled. Buy one large container rather than multiple small containers of the same thing. Some products are wrapped up in layers of unnecessary packaging—for example, a box of chocolates or an Easter egg. This packaging helps to sell the product, but it is just thrown away. This is a complete waste of resources, so try to avoid products with excess packaging. Fruits and vegetables often come in layers of packaging, too, so it is much better to buy from places where the produce is sold loose.

There are many one-use products on sale, such as single-use cameras, disposable flatware, paper plates, and so on. Once these products have been used, they are thrown away and new ones are purchased. Avoid these products and pay a little more for something that you can use many times instead.

When making decisions between two similar items, look to see if there is information about the recycled content. Try, wherever possible, to buy items made from recycled materials. Another choice would be to avoid those items that are difficult to recycle.

It may seem as if you are saving money by buying a cheaper product, but think about how long the product will last. It may be possible that a slightly more expensive item will last longer.

Finally, if you do not think a manufacturer is doing enough to cut waste, find out where the company is based and write to ask about the company's plans to cut waste.

Computers cannot easily be recycled because they contain harmful chemicals. When you're buying a new computer, think about whether you really need a new one, and also about what happens to your old one.

Glossary

acid rain rain made acidic by polluting gases in the atmosphere, such as sulfur dioxide; acid rain harms trees and water supplies, and damages buildings

alloy a chemical mix of two elements, one of which is a metal

biogas the name given to the mix of gases produced by rotting organic matter; biogas can be used as a fuel

consumable items items that are meant to be used up and replaced

consumer goods goods purchased for personal use—for example, televisions, computers, and refrigerators

coolant a liquid or gas used to cool a system by transferring heat away from one part to another

cullet crushed or broken glass for recycling

durability being hard-wearing; a durable product will last a long time

emission a substance, such as gas, given off or discharged; carbon dioxide, for example, is an emission produced by the burning of fossil fuels such as coal

fossil fuel a substance, such as coal, oil, or gas, that is formed from the decomposition of plant and animal remains; fossil fuels release carbon dioxide when they are burned

functionality how well something works

global warming the gradual rise in temperature over all of Earth's surface

impurity something that reduces the value of a substance

incinerator a place where waste can be burned

ingot a block of metal

landfill a large hole in the ground used to dump waste

malleable capable of being shaped or burned

molten made into a liquid by heating

ore a mineral from which a metal can be extracted

organic derived from living organisms

ozone a chemical found high in the atmosphere that filters out harmful ultraviolet rays from sunlight

pesticide a chemical used by farmers to control insect pests in their fields or on their livestock

pollutant a substance that causes pollution

quarry a place where rock is obtained from the ground by digging, cutting, or blasting

raw material the basic material from which a product is made; oil is one of the raw materials of plastic

recycle processing old, used items in order that the material can be used to make new products

refurbish to repair something to bring it back into good working order

resource an asset or material that is valuable; the world's natural resources include water and fossil fuels such as coal, gas, and oil

retardant a chemical that slows something down—for example, chemicals that slow down the spread of a fire

sanitation provision of clean drinking water and adequate disposal of sewage (human waste)

silt fine sand, clay, or other materials that are carried by water and often deposited in streams and rivers

textile a type of material made from fibers

toxic poisonous

vapor a type of gas

versatile able to adapt or be adapted to many different uses

Further information

Web sites

Friends of the Earth

http://www.foe.org

Environmental conservation organization that has a detailed Web site covering many environmental topics, including issues associated with waste and recycling.

United States Environmental Protection Agency

http://www.epa.gov/osw

Lots of information on all types of waste, laws, what you can do, and links to other sites.

Waste Online

http://www.wasteonline.org.uk

A comprehensive Web site looking at all forms of recycling, with facts and figures, information sheets, and suggestions on how to recycle more.

Plastics Recycling

http://www.plasticsrecycling.info

Web site that gives lots of information about plastics, how they are made and used, and how they can be recycled.

World Wise Waste Guide

http://www.worldwise.com/wiseguide.html

This Web site has an online resource guide to help you understand more about sustainable living, with information on recycling and buying environmentally friendly products.

Glass Packaging Institute

http://www.gpi.org/recycling/

Provides information about glass containers, including glass recycling facts and resources.

Fun Recycling Facts

http://www.resourcefulschools.org/html/facts.html

Web site with lots of recycling facts and a fun recycling trivia challenge game.

Global Stewards

http://www.globalstewards.org/main.htm

Offers tips on how we can all reduce, reuse, and recycle more of our garbage.

Books

Bowden, Rob. *Waste*. San Diego: Kidhaven Press, 2004.

Chandler, Gary. *Recycling*. New York: 21st Century Books, 1996.

Ganeri, Anita. *Something Old, Something New: Recycling*. Chicago: Heinemann Library, 2005.

Green, Jen. *Waste and Recycling*. North Mankato, Minn.: Chrysalis Education, 2004.

Kouhoupt, Rudy. *How on Earth Do We Recycle Metal?* Brookfield, Conn.: Millbrook Press, 1992.

Parker, Steve. *Textiles*. Milwaukee, Wis.: Gareth Stevens, 2002.

Smith, Heather. *Earth-friendly Crafts for Kids: 50 Awesome Things to Make with Recycled Stuff*. New York: Lark Books, 2002.

Woods, Samuel. *Recycled Paper: From Start to Finish*. Woodbridge, Conn.: Blackbirch Press, 2000.

Index